Cover Foreground, © Mike Powell/Allsport; Cover Background, © K. Chiang/Superstock

MERRILL READING PROGRAM

I CAN

FIFTH EDITION

Based on the philosophy of Charles C. Fries

Authors

Phyllis Bertin
Educational Coordinator
Windward School
White Plains, New York

Dr. Cecil D. Mercer
Professor of Education
University of Florida
Gainesville, Florida

Eileen Perlman
Learning Disabilities Specialist
White Plains Public Schools
White Plains, New York

Mildred K. Rudolph

Rosemary G. Wilson

SRA McGraw-Hill

Columbus, Ohio

A Division of The McGraw·Hill Companies

TABLE OF CONTENTS

SRA/McGraw-Hill

A Division of The McGraw-Hill Companies

Send all inquiries to:
SRA/McGraw-Hill
8787 Orion Place
Columbus, Ohio 43240-4027

ISBN 0-02-674706-5

8 9 10 BCH 06 05

cat

fat

Nat

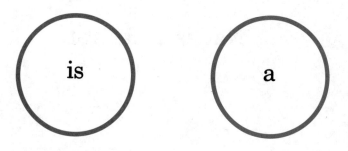

| cat fat | fat Nat | Nat cat | fat cat Nat |

A Cat

Nat is a cat.

Nat is fat.

Nat is a fat cat.

Nat

Is Nat a cat?

Nat is a cat.

Nat is a fat cat.

A Fat Cat

Nat is a cat.

Is Nat fat?

Nat is fat.

Nat is a fat cat.

cat

fat

Nat

pat

mat

sat

the

on

| cat pat | fat mat | Nat sat | mat pat |

Fat Nat

A cat sat on a mat.

Pat the cat.

Is the cat Nat?

The cat is fat Nat.

Pat Nat on the mat.

A Cat on a Mat

Is a cat on a mat?

A cat is on a mat.

Is the cat fat?

The cat is fat.

Is the cat Nat?

The cat on the mat is Nat.

Nat on the Mat

A fat cat sat on a mat.

The fat cat is Nat.

Pat Nat, the fat cat.

Is the mat on Nat?

Nat is on the mat.

cat

fat

Nat

pat

mat

sat

hat

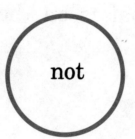

not

fat hat	cat sat	mat hat	pat hat

A Hat on a Cat

A cat is on a mat.

Pat the cat.

Is a hat on the cat?

A hat is on the cat.

Nat on a Hat

Nat! Nat!

Pat the hat.

Nat sat on the hat.

Is the hat on Nat?

The hat is not on Nat.

Nat is on the hat.

A Hat on the Cat

The cat is on a mat.

A hat is on the cat.

Is the hat on the mat?

The hat is not on the mat.

Is the cat on the hat?

The cat is not on the hat.

The hat is on the cat.

cat

fat

Nat

pat

mat

sat

hat

bat

at

look

he

| fat bat | bat at | hat bat | at sat |

On the Hat

Nat! Nat!

Look at the hat!

The hat is on the mat.

Pat the hat, Nat.

Nat sat on the hat.

The Bat

Look at the bat, Nat.

The bat is on the mat.

Nat sat on the bat.

Is Nat on the mat?

He is on the mat.

Is Nat on the bat?

He is on the bat.

Look at Nat

Look at Nat.

He is a cat.

Pat Nat, the fat cat.

Look at the hat.

The hat is on the cat.

The hat is on fat Nat.

can

man

ran

Dan

Jan

cat	mat	can	ran
can	man	man	Jan
		ran	Dan

Jan at Bat

Jan is at bat.

Can Jan bat?

Jan can bat.

Look at Jan bat.

Jan ran.

Look! Jan is at the mat.

Dan

Is a man at bat?

A man is not at bat.

Dan is at bat.

Can Dan bat?

He can bat.

Dan ran.

Pat Nat

Dan, look at the cat.

Look at fat Nat.

Can Dan pat the fat cat?

He can pat Nat.

Can Jan pat Nat?

Jan can pat the cat.

A Hat on Dan

Look at the hat.

The hat is not on Nat.

The hat is not on a man.

Is the hat on Dan?

The hat is on Dan.

Look at Jan

Look at Dan.

Is he at bat?

Dan is not at bat.

Jan is at bat.

Look at Jan bat.

Jan ran.

can

man

ran

Dan

Jan

fan

pan

van

(to)   (in)

| fat fan | pat pan | man fan pan | fan pan van |

Nat at the Fan

A fan is in the van.

Nat is at the fan.

The fan is not on.

Dan ran the fan.

Nat ran.

The Pan

Look at the pan.

The pan is on a mat.

Look at Nat.

Nat ran to the pan.

Nat is on the mat.

A Man in a Van

Look at the van, Jan.

A man is in the van.

Jan ran to the van.

Dan ran to the van.

The man ran the van.

Dan is not in the van.

Jan is not in the van.

On the Van

Is Nat in the van?

Nat is not in the van.

He is on the van.

Jan sat in the van.

Nat! Nat!

Not on the van!

Nat ran to Jan in the van.

In the Van

The man ran the van.

Dan is in the van.

Nat is not in the van.

Nat ran to the van.

Nat sat on Dan.

Dan can pat Nat in the van.

cap

lap

nap

Dan's

Jan's

see   her

cat	Nat	cap	Dan
cap	nap	nap	Dan's
		lap	Jan's

On Jan's Lap

A cat is on Jan's lap.

See the cat on her lap?

Is the cat Nat?

Nat is the cat on Jan's lap.

Jan can pat Nat.

Nat can nap on her lap.

Jan's Cap

A cap is on Jan's lap.

The cap is Jan's cap.

Nat can see the cap.

Nat ran to bat the cap.

The cap is not on Jan's lap.

The cap is on the mat.

A Cap on a Mat

Look at Dan's cap.

The cap is on a mat.

Nat ran to bat the cap.

Dan! Dan!

Look at Nat bat the cap.

Dan ran to see Nat.

Cat on a Lap

Nat sat on Jan's lap.

Jan's cap is on her lap.

Nat sat on her cap.

Is Nat on Jan's cap?

Nat is on Jan's cap.

A Nap on a Lap

Jan sat on a mat.

Nat ran to Jan.

He sat on Jan's lap.

Nat can nap on Jan's lap.

See Nat on Jan's lap?

Look at the cat nap.

cap

lap

nap

map

tap

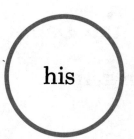

his

| mat
man
map | Nat
nap | cap
lap
tap | map
tap
nap |

Dan's Nap

Dan sat on his mat.

Dan can nap on the mat.

Nat can see Dan on the mat.

He ran to Dan.

Nat can tap Dan.

Can Dan nap?

The Cap

Nat can see Jan's cap.

Nat ran to bat the cap.

The cap is on the mat.

Nat ran to his mat.

Nat can tap the cap.

See Nat tap Jan's cap.

Jan's cap is not on the mat.

A Cat Can

Can a cat nap?

Nat can nap.

A cat can nap.

Can a cat tap?

Nat can tap Jan.

A cat can tap.

Jan's Map

A man is in a van.

Jan sat in the van.

A map is on her lap.

Look at the map, Jan.

Jan can look at her map.

The man ran his van.

A Cat on a Map

A cat sat on a map.

The cat is Nat.

Nat! Nat!

Not on the map!

Nat sat on Jan's lap.

Dad

Dad's

had

bad

Nat's

she

hat had	bat bad	had bad Dad	Dad Dad's Nat's

A Bad Nap

Look at Dan.

He is on a mat.

Dan had a bad nap.

He ran to Nat.

Nat is on his lap.

Dan can pat Nat.

Look, Dad

Jan's cap is on Nat's mat.

Nat is on her cap.

Look, Dad!

Nat is on Jan's cap.

Is Nat a bad cat?

Dad's Hat

Look at Dad's hat, Jan.

His hat is on Nat's mat.

Jan ran to look at the hat.

Nat had Dad's hat.

Jan ran to Dad.

Is Nat a bad cat?

Nat's Nap

Dad's hat is on Nat's mat.

Nat can not nap on the mat.

Nat can see Dad.

He ran to Dad.

Dad had a nap.

Nat had a nap on Dad's lap.

Dad, Jan, Nat

Dad had a bat.

He had a fan.

He had a hat.

Jan had a cap.

She had a cat.

She had a map.

Nat had a pan.

He had a mat.

He had a can.

Dad

Dad's

had

bad

mad

sad

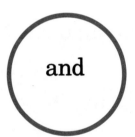

and

sat sad	hat had	bat bad	mat map mad

Is Dad Sad?

Jan and Dan had a cat.

The cat is Nat.

Nat sat on Dad's hat.

Is Nat bad?

Is Dad mad at Nat?

Dad is not mad.

He is sad.

Nat's Pan

Nat's pan is in the van.

Nat is sad.

He ran to Dan.

Dan ran to the van.

He can see the pan.

Dan had the pan.

Nat is not sad.

Jan's Bat, Cap, and Pan

Jan had a bat.

Her bat is on a mat.

Jan had a cap.

Her cap is on her lap.

Jan had a pan.

Her pan is in the van.

A Bad Cat

Jan and Dan had a bad cat.

Nat is the bad cat.

He had Dad's map.

Dad is sad.

Nat had Jan's cap.

Jan is mad.

Dad is sad.

Jan is mad.

Is Nat bad?

Is Nat Bad?

Nat had a nap on Dan's cap.

Look at his cap!

Is Dan mad at Nat?

He is mad at Nat.

Is Nat bad?

Bad cat!

He can nap on his mat.

ham

jam

Sam

Sam's

am

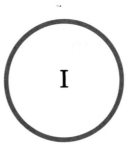

at am	hat had ham	sat Sam Sam's	ham Sam jam

Sam

Sam is the man in the van.

Sam sat in his van.

He had a ham in a pan.

Jan ran to see Sam.

Jan and Sam had ham.

I Am Sam

I am Sam.

I ran the van.

I had to look at a map.

Nat had the map.

He is not in the van.

The map is not in the van.

I am mad at Nat.

A Nap on Sam's Map

I am Nat, a fat cat.

I had a nap on Sam's map.

Sam had to look at the map.

He is sad.

I am sad.

I am not bad, am I?

Am I Sam?

I am not Dan.

I am not Jan.

I am not Dad.

I am not Nat, the fat cat.

I ran the van.

Am I Sam?

Sam's Jam

Sam had jam in a can.

Nat can see Sam's jam.

He ran to bat the can.

Nat can tap and bat the can.

The jam is not in the can.

The jam is on Nat!

bag

rag

tag

wag

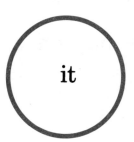

it

| bat bad bag | tap tag | ran rag | rag tag wag |

Nat's Nap

Sam had a rag in the van.

Nat ran to nap on it.

Nat can nap on a rag.

He can nap on a mat.

Can he nap on a bag?

Tag the Bag

Jan is at bat.

She can tap on the mat.

She can bat.

Jan ran and ran.

She had to tag the bag.

Dan ran to tag Jan.

She is on the bag.

Tag—Tap—Wag

Can a man tag a bag?

Sam is a man.

He can tag a bag.

Can Dan tap a pan?

Dan had a pan.

He can tap on his pan.

Can a cat wag?

Nat can wag at Jan.

A cat can wag.

Nat and the Ham

Sam had a ham in a bag.

Nat can see the bag.

Nat ran to the bag.

He can bat it.

The bag is a rag!

Nat! Bad cat!

The ham is Sam's.

Nat and Dan's Hat

Dan's hat is in a bag.

Nat ran to the bag.

Nat can bat the bag.

He can tap the hat.

He sat on it.

Look at Dan's hat.

It is a rag!

Dan is sad.

bats

pats

taps

maps

bags

wags

rags   Rags

tap	bag	rags	wag
taps	bags	Rags	wags

Rags

I am fat.

I am not a cat.

I can wag and wag.

I can nap on a mat.

I am Rags.

Sam and Rags

Sam is in the van.

Rags is on his lap.

Sam pats Rags.

She wags at Sam.

Sam ran the van.

Rags had a nap.

Sam and Dan

Dan ran to the van.

Sam is in the van.

Dan taps on the van.

He had Sam's maps.

Sam can look at the maps.

He ran the van.

Rags and Nat

Look at Rags and Nat.

Rags and Nat ran.

Rags ran to the van.

She ran to Jan and Dan.

Nat ran to Dad.

Dad had ham in a pan.

Rags had a nap.

Nat had ham.

Nat's Nap

Jan had bags and rags.

She had maps in the bags.

Nat had a nap on the bags.

Jan is mad.

Bad Nat, to nap on the bags!

Not on the maps, Nat.

Nap on the rags.

He had a nap on Jan's rags.

A Nap on a Mat

Rags had a nap on Nat's mat.

Nat bats at Rags.

Rags is sad.

She ran to Sam.

Sam pats Rags.

Rags is not sad.

Jan's Ham

Jan had a bag.

She had a ham in it.

Nat and Rags ran to look.

Nat is a bad cat.

He bats the ham.

Rags is not bad.

She wags and wags.

Rags and Dad

Dad had a nap.

Rags is sad.

She taps and taps on Dad.

Dad can see Rags.

He can see her bat a cap.

She bats Dad's hat.

Rags wags and wags.

Dad pats Rags.

Rags is not sad.

TO THE TEACHER

The MERRILL READING PROGRAM consists of eight Readers developed on linguistic principles applicable to the teaching of reading. The rationale of the program and detailed teaching procedures are described in the Teacher's Edition of each Reader.

Instant recognition and identification of the letters of the alphabet must be developed before beginning instruction in *I CAN.* The practice needed for alphabet mastery is provided in *MY ALPHABET BOOK.*

All words introduced in this Reader are listed on the next page under the headings "Words in Pattern" and "Sight Words."

Words listed as "Words in Pattern" represent six groups of words in the first major set of spelling patterns. These words have the matrixes *-at, -an, -ap, -ad, -am,* and *-ag.* With the exception of *at* and *am,* each word in each group begins with a different consonant letter. These initial consonant letters provide the contrastive features by which the printed words are distinguished from each other and recognized. The initial consonant letters introduced in this Reader are *b, c, d, f, h, j, l, m, n, p, r, s, t, v,* and *w.* In addition, some pattern pages present pattern words with the endings *-s* and *-'s.*

Words listed as "Sight Words" are high-frequency words introduced to provide normal sentence patterns in the stories.